The Rest of the Story

The Rest of the Story

◆

Branches From Our Tree

Howard D. Henderson
&
Jean Dryden Henderson

iUniverse, Inc.
New York Lincoln Shanghai

The Rest of the Story
Branches From Our Tree

iUniverse books may be ordered through booksellers or by contacting:

iUniverse
2021 Pine Lake Road, Suite 100
Lincoln, NE 68512
www.iuniverse.com
1-800-Authors (1-800-288-4677)

ISBN-13: 978-0-595-37791-6 (pbk)
ISBN-13: 978-0-595-82166-2 (ebk)
ISBN-10: 0-595-37791-2 (pbk)
ISBN-10: 0-595-82166-9 (ebk)

Printed in the United States of America

Merry Christmas 2005!

We are so excited to be able to put your past, our family, and your stories into a book that will always mean so much to all of us. Thank you so much for putting your words down on paper.

We Love You!

Sue & Wayne,
Kirk & Terri,
Jane & Stan,
Amy, Jeff & Owen,
Brian, Kim,
and Heidi, Chris, & Julia

"…and now you know…the Rest of the Story."

—Paul Harvey

Contents

Jean…

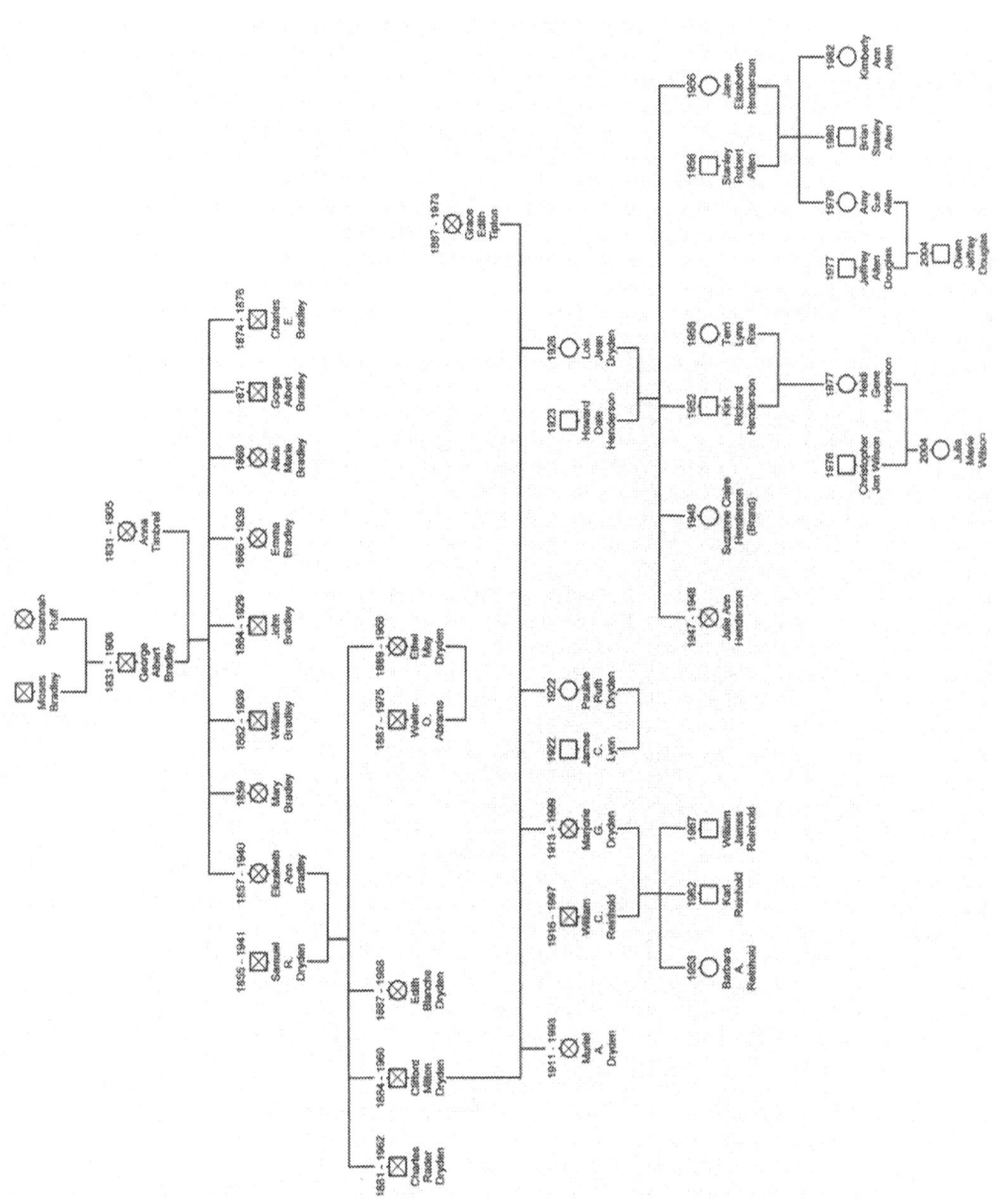

This family photo was taken in the early 1930's. It is the Dryden family. Grandpa and Grandma lived at 1111 W. 22nd Street in Cedar Falls, Iowa. They retired from farming in the Montezuma area in southern Iowa.

We are in the backyard. Grandpa still had the chicken coop with lots of chickens. A few years later, Aunt Edith landscaped the yard (no more chickens). She created a lovely setting—grass, flowers, trees, bushes and a fireplace made of flagstone for cooking. Her pride and joy were her tulip beds.

The photo occasion was a visit of my father's brother Charles, his wife Verna and son James…a rare event since Charlie lived in Idaho.

All of Sam and Elizabeth Dryden's children are pictured—Clifford, Charlie, Edith, and Ethel.

Standing in the back row: Muriel Dryden (my sister), Uncle Charles Dryden, his son James, Grace Dryden (my mother), Grandpa Sam Dryden, Edith Dryden, Charlie's wife Verna and Uncle Abe

Seated on the bench: Marjorie (my sister), Polly (my sister), my Dad, Clifford Dryden, Grandma Elizabeth Dryden with me on her lap

On the ground: Aunt Ethel Abrams and her daughter Anne

Samuel & Elizabeth Dryden at their home on 1111 22nd Street,
Cedar Falls, Iowa in 1936

I Remember Lincoln School in the 1930's

by

Jean Dryden Henderson

Foreword

Written May 2004
by Heidi Henderson Wilson

As the closing of Lincoln Elementary at 942 Newton Street was approaching, this story was shared with a fifth grade class at Lincoln School. As described in an article in the Sunday, May 2, 2004, edition of the *Waterloo-Cedar Falls Courier*, my Grandma, Jean Dryden Henderson was able to visit this fifth grade class. She shared many of the differences and similarities that exist in the classroom today compared to when she was at Lincoln School in the 1930's. The students were very interested in learning more about what her time in school was like and prepared these questions for her visit. I believe my Grandma and the students enjoyed the experience very much.

1. What was the playground like?

2. What was PE (Physical Education) like?

3. How did the students act?

4. Were all the teachers nice?

5. Did you have recess? How long?

6. What subjects did you learn?

7. What was the classroom like?

8. How many students were in the school?

9. What was the time of the school day?

10. How long was your lunch break at home?

11. What would happen if you got in trouble?

12. Did some students take the bus home?

13. What was your best subject? Worst?

14. What did students wear?

15. Did you have chalkboards?

16. What did you write with and on?

17. Was your hand print on the wall?

I have always enjoyed working on projects with my Grandma. I treasured helping her compile these memories into a piece of literature that will give her grandchildren and their children insight into whom their Grandma was before she started her own family. Now that I am preparing to have a child, I think turning as much of our family history into something tangible has become even more important.

I love you, Grandma,
Heidi

I Remember Lincoln School
in the 1930's

Mr. Miller, the custodian, lived across the street from the school. Two of his duties were raising and lowering the flag each day and ringing a hand-held bell while standing outside in the schoolyard.

It was our signal to go inside. Upon entering, we could hear our principal's Victrola playing a John Phillips Sousa march, "The Liberty Bell March." Miss Carl greeted us as we marched up the steps to our various rooms, younger students to the first floor, older students to the second. The music was stimulating.

I started at Lincoln in January 1931. My birthday was December 5th. I have yet in my memory that birthday. I had greatly anticipated turning five. I had the idea upon awakening that I would have grown taller. I was greatly disappointed. I had not grown.

I was a midyear student starting kindergarten in January. The first semester we went only mornings, the second semester only afternoons. When we were promoted to first grade, the first semester we joined the class which was one semester ahead of us. The second semester we joined the class which was one semester behind us. The first semester we were identified as being in, B and the second semester as being, A.

This system continues through 7th grade. I liked this change of class-mates as we became well acquainted and learned from both groups.

First of all, I need to say how very fortunate we students of Lincoln were. Our teachers were outstanding. They offered a stimulating education during the depression years of the 1930's. The fathers of many students had no jobs. Somehow during that period, Lincoln School District remained surprisingly stable.

The school provided a center of interest. Parents attended and took part in P.T.A. meetings. For example, my father sang "The Old Oaken Bucket" * in a quartet. My friend Beth's mother played basketball in the gym in the evening with other mothers.

As an award for parents' attendance to P.T.A., a picture of Abraham Lincoln traveled from room to room. Students were quite proud when their room was a winner.

* "The Old Oaken Bucket" is considered to be the most famous poem of Samuel Woodworth, (1784-1842). This poem is best known in its musical setting.

THE OLD OAKEN BUCKET
Samuel Woodworth

How dear to this heart are the scenes of my childhood,
When fond recollections present them to view!
The orchard, the meadow, the deep-tangled wild wood,
And every loved spot which my infancy knew;
The wide-spreading pond, and the mill which stood by it,
The bridge and the rock where the cataract fell;
The cot of my father, the dairy house nigh it,
And e'en the rude bucket which hung in the well;
The old oaken bucket, the iron-bound bucket,
The moss-cover'd bucket, which hung in the well.

That moss-cover'd vessel I hail as a treasure;
For often, at noon, when return'd from the field,
I found it the source of an exquisite pleasure,
The purest and sweetest that Nature can yield.
How ardent I seized it, with hands that were glowing!
And quick to the white-pebbled bottom it fell;
Then soon, with the emblem of truth overflowing,
And dripping with coolness, it rose from the well;
The old oaken bucket, the iron-bound bucket,
The moss-cover'd bucket arose from the well.

How sweet from the green mossy brim to receive it,
As poised on the curb it inclined to my lips!
Not a full blushing goblet could tempt me to leave it,
Though fill'd with the nectar that Jupiter sips.
And now, far removed from the loved situation,
The tear of regret will intrusively swell,
As fancy reverts to my father's plantation,
And sighs for the bucket which hangs in the well;
The old oaken bucket, the iron-bound bucket,
The moss-cover'd bucket, which hangs in the well.

KINDERGARTEN
Miss Itnyre

Miss Itnyre taught colors using yarn balls. She also taught us to tie shoelaces. Since I already knew colors and how to tie shoelaces, I helped other students.

There were play stations, a sand table in the cloak room, a block corner and dolls and furniture to play "house".

We loved sitting on the floor near the piano to sing and to listen to Miss Itnyre read, showing us the pictures in the books she read to us.

We had many chances to draw, cut, and paste. It was a calm atmosphere providing us with a good start.

FIRST GRADE
Miss Horsch & Miss Jensen

We started reading in first grade. I recall a flash card with "MILK" printed on it. Our first word.

I don't know if it was only our class, but we were not taught to sound our words from the spelling. Later on in junior high and high school, teachers would tell us to sound out a difficult word. They were surprised we had no idea how to do it.

The district school nurse visited Lincoln periodically. I specifically recall her looking us over in first grade. We lined up by the window so she could check our faces, hands, and ears and then look down our throats using a flashlight. Next she took two clean toothpicks from a box, pushed our hair aside and looked at our scalp. I realized years later that she was looking for head lice!

I was disciplined by Miss Jensen. One day I wore a new dress with a belt and a neat buckle. I took the belt off and on several times, playing with the buckle. I was sent to the cloakroom. I must have annoyed her!

SECOND GRADE
Miss Watson

I have no memory of second grade. Looking at my report card, I was absent *a lot*. No doubt that is when I had measles and chicken pox. Even so, my grades were above average. I do know this was the time I made a discovery. If it was a cloudy day and the teacher turned on the light in the school room, I loved the atmosphere it created. A contentment came over me. This continued all through grade school when these conditions existed.

THIRD GRADE
Miss Baird—a favorite

Miss Baird was gifted with the ability to inspire her students.

During this year, we studied pioneer life and Indian lore. Miss Baird led us through the process of building a tepee. We started with long slender sticks tied together at the top and spread out at the bottom. Some of us brought flour sacks from home and sewed them together. Next we dyed them using the green outer shells of walnuts. We dried the tent fabric by spreading it out on the grass. When dry, we wrapped it around the frame of sticks. We had an opening flap for a doorway. The tepee probably wasn't as large as it seemed then, but we could get inside it.

Lincoln School Waterloo ~ 3rd. Grade ~ Jan. 1936

Miss Baird was responsible for our first performance in costume. She selected four girls and four boys to dance the minuet. My friend, Beth recalls Miss Baird asking her to go downstairs to the gym to help her work out the steps in the dance. She knew that Beth was taking dancing lessons. We performed for a women's group at the YWCA. Of the eight dancers, I recall only Marilyn, Beth, Bob Myers and Eugene Beightol.

Our mothers made the rather elaborate costumes, girls in pink, boys in blue. We looked like George and Martha Washington with our wigs made of cotton, totally covering our heads.

The dance started with 1-2-3 and point your toe, etc. We danced the minuet. We did do a performance at P.T.A. so our parents could see us.

We started cursive writing in third grade. We were taught the Palmer method. We practiced doing push-pulls and ovals. You rotated your hand and arm as you wrote. It was bad enough using a pencil, but when we were advanced to using those scratchy ink pens made up of a 702 pen point, stuck into a wooden holder, it was ridiculous. However, we all survived and several of my friends developed beautiful penmanship!

MOVING UPSTAIRS

Grades fourth through seventh were on the second floor. Our daily routine changed considerably. We actually acquired four new teachers. We spent a portion of the day with each of the teachers in four different rooms.

Our principal, Miss Carl, was replaced by Mrs. Grupp about this time.

Mrs. Grupp, principal

FOURTH GRADE
Miss Packer

Miss Packer taught social studies. There was a large map of the United States hanging in her room. My memory is limited to learning the names of the states, the crops grown, and their natural resources.

Miss Packer had a distracting habit of wrapping and unwrapping a rubber band around her fingers.

FIFTH GRADE
Miss Bailey

Miss Bailey taught English and Science. Her classes were so interesting. We watched the Monarch butterfly emerge from a chrysalis and learned the constellations. Marilyn and I especially enjoyed searching the skies when she slept over on our screened front porch during hot summer nights.

Our class published a Lincoln newspaper, taking turns being the editor.

We learned parliamentary procedure by forming a science club.

SIXTH GRADE
Miss Hadley

Miss Hadley's was a great personality and her figure was a curiosity to us. She had very wide hips, wore wide belts around a fairly narrow waist.

Marilyn, Beth, and I enjoyed visiting with her after school. We were good students in her arithmetic and spelling classes. At times we were asked to help a few students with their studies.

Remarkably, Miss Hadley taught us about loan interest rates. We were warned to be alert as to whether interest rates were calculated monthly or annually in financing a home.

During the depression, there were many loan companies loaning money at unreasonable rates.

SEVENTH GRADE
Miss Oagle and Miss Knowles

They taught art, music & literature, and physical training

I felt quite at home in this classroom. In thinking back, these teachers had to be the busiest of all.

We were exposed to all well known artists and their paintings. My favorites at that time were *The Blue Boy* and *Pinkie*.

Miss Bradbury came to our building periodically. She supervised an elaborate chalk drawing on the blackboard.

We must have been reading about "The Knights of the Round Table". The subject of the drawing was Sir Galahad on horseback, approaching a castle. Arnold Robertson and Eugene Border were assigned to drawing the horses and rider, I helped with the castle.

Music appreciation was great. We heard "In the Hall of the Mountain King" often and it appealed to the whole class. In singing class, we were taught to sing harmony, boys and girls alike. I don't believe the boys voices had changed yet.

Talent programs were held, at least once a year fourth through seventh grades. Of course we violin players performed, Marilyn, Louise, Doris Lee and I. A couple of boys played various horns. Beth and Marilyn played piano solos. Beth also did some ballet. Arnold Robertson sang "Fairest Lord Jesus" to perfection. Constance Oleson played guitar and Andrew Price played his Juice Harp. I am certain many more students than I remember, also performed.

Along with the regular duties in the department, Miss Oagle and Miss Knowles had the huge responsibility of preparing students at Lincoln to perform in productions held at East High. These events were made up of students representing each of the grade schools in the East side district.

Miss Collyer was in charge of physical training and Miss Gaiser was the music director. These teachers visited each grade school teaching and coordinating the events.

I have included notes of each of the performances our class was involved in. I have no dates as to when they occurred or the proper order in which they were held. Marilyn, Beth, and I performed in all of them, adding another bond to our friendship.

Performances

In "Jack & The Magic Beanstalk," we sang in the chorus, wearing villager costumes. I recall a laced bodice dress. We sang:

"His ho maidens and men will dance on the green in the morning. Spring is here, day is clear…

In another performance, we wore Dutch costumes, both boys and girls in blue. Girls wore Dutch hats; we all wore wooden shoes. We danced and sang:

"The Dutch boys and girls live in Holland. They're as happy as happy can be."

There were also two physical training demonstrations at East High, rope jumping and tumbling.

Costumes

Starting with the Minuet costumes in the third grade, followed by a villager costume, a Dutch costume, outfits to wear in rope jumping and tumbling, and a costume for the May Festival, I realize now, why my mother started saying, "What do you want to do that for?" She made all of my costumes!

My Goodness. Mrs. DuBois certainly went to great lengths.

Marilyn in her Villager Costume

Marilyn's Brother Jim in his Pirate's Costume and Marilyn in her Dutch
Costume

Marilyn and I

From the first time in Kindergarten, Marilyn and I started a relationship that would last a lifetime.

Marilyn lived at 803 Riehl; I was at 827 Dawson. Marilyn came by my house everyday on the way to school. If I wasn't ready, she stopped in and waited for me. I lived four blocks from school, Marilyn lived one block beyond.

We came home for lunch; we always walked. Maybe that is why we are still, at age 77, physically strong ladies. The WCF&N[1] railroad tracks were right next to my house. We used to say we were learning good posture by walking on those rails and we did it a lot!

During those eight years attending Lincoln, we had many routes to get there. We would discuss it, "Shall we take Dawson to Avon to Newton or the railroad track to Kern then the alley to Newton?"

If we needed to buy pencils, tablets (Big Chief or my favorite, a Goldenrod) or a 702 pen point, we walked down Dawson to Burton, to Tommy's grocery store. We stayed on the left side of the street to head on

---

1. Waterloo, Cedar Falls & Northern. The WCF&N provided a daily link between the small communities, such as LaPorte City, with Waterloo. It brought residents of the small farming towns into contact with big city schools, businesses and way of life. It provided a way to ship produce and for people to travel to Waterloo for shopping, and a way for Catholic children to have access to the Catholic school located in Waterloo. The company was founded as a Waterloo horse car line in 1895. By 1914 it extended from Cedar Rapids to Waverly, with both freight and passenger service powered by electricity. Passengers could make the 60-mile trip from Waterloo to Cedar Rapids in 1917 in an hour and 45 minutes. Freight took approximately three hours over the same route. The WCF&N continued its passenger service between Waterloo and Cedar Rapids until 1956. The company eventually became part of the Illinois Central Railroad, which later abandoned the track between Waterloo and Cedar Rapids.

to school. I was not fond of walking near the tombstones that were sold across the street from the store.

During all those walks to and from school, we shared our thoughts and happenings at school, our homes and our churches. We could talk endlessly. Once in awhile we disagreed, each going our separate ways home. We were so miserable when this happened that either my mother or Marilyn's talked us into phoning the other. All was forgotten. Our mothers used the expression "chums" to describe us.

Beth was also with us a good share of the time from third grade on. The three of us formed the "Black Magic Club." We tried unsuccessfully to recruit other friends at school to join this fascinating club. We finally gave up.

Marilyn, Beth and I met regularly at each other's homes. We held our meetings, going through rituals that we are still unable to reveal. This was truly one of the highlights of our childhood. Our sense of mystery had no doubt been stimulated by the series of Nancy Drew books we read.

There was one person we could have recruited very easily, Marilyn's brother, Jim. But heaven forbid, we couldn't do that. He was a *boy*—horrors!

In third grade, Marilyn and I chose to have violin lessons when they were offered at school. Paul Smith, a friend of Marilyn's family and Wesley Eagen, a member of the church I attended were quite accomplished violin players. We were inspired by them.

I made quite a scene when my parents refused to purchase a violin for me. My sister, Muriel came to my rescue. She gave me a half size violin with a lovely tone.

Muriel was employed at the Visiting Nursing Association. She was fifteen years my senior and truly a fine big sister. She played a cello in the Waterloo Symphony. That explains her understanding of my desire to play an instrument.

Marilyn, Louise Kern, Doris Lee Murphy and I had a darling teacher, Eunice Ryan. Our lessons were held in the gym once a week, third grade through seventh grade.

The first piece of music we memorized was "Twinkle, Twinkle Little Star." Marilyn and I regretted that orchestras didn't march as bands did. On one occasion we marched up and down the gym playing "Twinkle, Twinkle Little Star," trying to prove to Eunice it could be done!

At some point, we were ready to play in the grade school orchestra which met for practice at East High each Saturday.

We rode the bus to and from East High. Buses were convenient for us. The Loop bus traveled on Riehl Street. It stopped at the railroad tracks and also in front of Marilyn's house. We became quite comfortable using the bus from then on.

I hesitate to mention some of the silly things we did to get attention during our practices at East High. Some students laughed at our antics, Roger Olesen always did. Eunice and Pauline Sutherland, our orchestra directors, must have decided they would just put up with us.

Beyond grade school, Marilyn and I moved easily into playing in the East Jr. High orchestra. There were concerts as in grade school, we also had sectional lessons. It was a fine program for learning an instrument.

When we reached East High, Marilyn lost interest, I continued on. Muriel had given me a full size violin by then and paid for private lessons with Miss Green, director of the East High Orchestra. Miss Green was an accomplished violinist. She taught me a lovely piece, "Mighty like a Rose," for a solo.

Besides playing in the East High Orchestra, I was invited to join a group of advanced students. We wore uniforms when we performed. I recall one of the pieces we performed, "Arrival of the Guests." Tenth grade was the first time since Jr. High in which Marilyn and I did not have lockers next to each other. My locker was in the music department.

I was at East High through grade 11B. My life was changed when my family moved to the west side of Waterloo. My orchestra days were over due to my lack of confidence to play in a new group.

Muriel was so hurt by my decision she immediately sold my violin. That was that. However, my appreciation for classical music had been developed, an appreciation that has lasted a lifetime.

My Sisters at Lincoln

Since my two older sisters are no longer living, I can't call them on the phone and say, "How long did you attend Lincoln?" The next best idea was to call my sister, Polly. We have agreed. Marjorie and Muriel each spent a few years there.

Polly was at Lincoln from Kindergarten through seventh. She also had the experience of performing in a grade school operetta at East High. It was entitled, "Polly Make Believe." She tried out for the lead role but was not chosen. However, she performed with the chorus. The girls from Lincoln wore costumes made of crepe paper. They were apple blossoms. Their song was "Blossom Time."

Yes of course, mother made the costume.

Smelly Shoes

This event could very well have happened as early as first grade. To begin with, my parents were very conservative in spending money wherever they could. After all, our country was going through a depression.

My father planted a fine vegetable garden. We had fruit trees and grapevines. My mother canned vegetables, made jams and jellies and catsup. The family called it Jeanne's catsup.

When it came to clothing, mother also made some of my wardrobe and being the youngest in a family of four girls, I also wore hand-me-downs.

So it was not unusual for my parents to have this plan for my white summer shoes. There was plenty of wear left in them and I surely would outgrow them by next year.

The solution was to dye the white shoes with black liquid dye. I don't recall any fuss made on my part. In fact, they looked very nice.

So I wore them to school. After sitting at my desk for awhile that morning, I started smelling something quite strong and unpleasant. The kids around me started sniffing and mumbling to each other about the odor.

All at once I realized it was my shoes! I was so embarrassed and humiliated. I finally went to the teacher, saying I was feeling very ill and wanted to go home, which I did.

It was never mentioned again at home or at school. I know I never wore dyed shoes again. My friend Marilyn's only remark to me about my sudden illness was, "You sure missed a good time at school. We got to go to the gym and watch a film put on by the Wonder Bakery." Darn!

Edward Sesser

1935

This photo of Edward was taken in our backyard. We are standing under the plum trees. Notice the railroad tracks so close to our yard. My beaded burlap dress and feathered headdress were made by my mother for a school occasion. She also made Edward's shirt and headdress. We liked to play Indians.

Edward lived a few houses from us on Dawson St. He was born with a heart condition. In preschool days, my mother took me to his house to entertain him. I liked this. He had the greatest toys, boy toys that we didn't have in our house of girls.

He started school at Lincoln. Being Catholic, the plan was for him to go to St. Mary's when he was able to ride his bike there. In fourth grade, he started doing the mile ride. He did it for a few weeks. It was too much for him. Soon after, the family moved close to St. Mary's. Our friendship waned, by our early teens, we lost touch.

Edward graduated from University of Iowa in 1949. On his drive home to Waterloo after commencement, he pulled his car off the highway and died of a heart attack.

Howard…

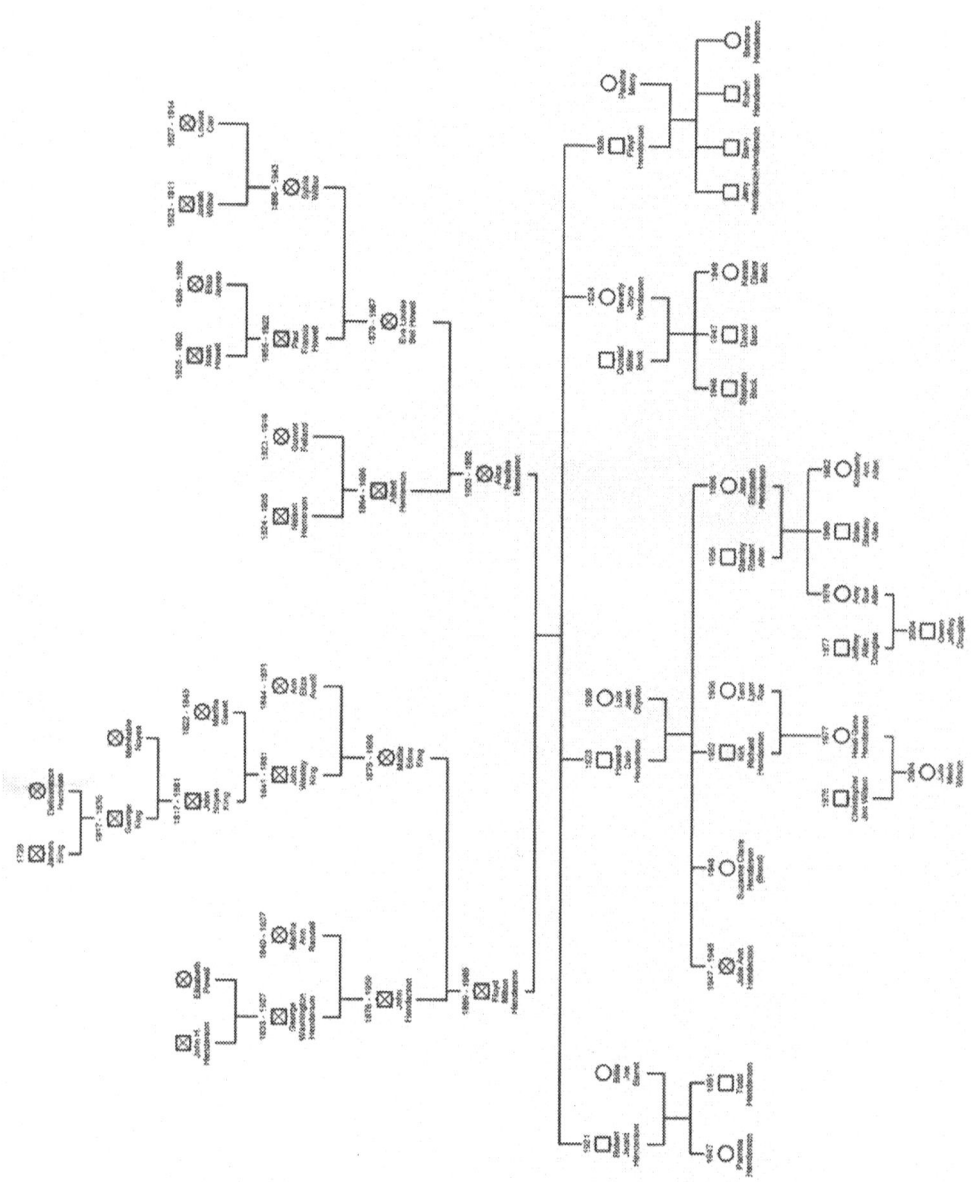

33

Row 1: Dean Madsen, Floyd Jr. Henderson, Beverly Henderson, Gene Madsen, Bob Henderson, Howard Henderson

Row 2: Great Grandma (Martha) Henderson, Grandpa (John) Henderson, Grandma (Mattie) Henderson, Alice Henderson (Howard's mother), Floyd Henderson (Howard's father), Lois Williams, Lucille Williams, Edna Madsen, John Madsen

HOWARD HENDERSON'S PARENTS

Floyd Milton Henderson

1899-1985

Born-Bradgate, IA

Died-Glendale, AZ

Buried-Glendale, AZ

Alice Pauline Hemerson

1903-1952

Born-Bradgate, IA

Died-Des Moines, IA

Buried-Waterloo, IA

Married March 29, 1921–Bradgate, IA
Floyd remarried to Theresa Bela in 1954
Two step-daughters—Judy & Vickie Bela

To Floyd & Alice three sons & one daughter were born all at Bradgate, IA Floyd & Alice Henderson moved their family to Waterloo, IA in 1929 where Floyd had secured employment at John Deere Tractor Works, where he worked 35 years until his retirement in 1964. Alice was employed at Rath Packing Co., during the 1930's depression years until a heart condition forced retirement. Robert, Howard, Beverly & Floyd Jr. all graduated from Waterloo West High School. Robert and Howard served in the armed forces of World War II.

HOWARD HENDERSON'S FATHER'S PATERNAL ANCESTRY—THE HENDERSONS

Howard's Paternal Great-Great Grandparents:
John H. and Elizabeth Powell Henderson

John was born in Kentucky-Elizabeth in North Carolina-Married in 1827—A son George Washington born in 1933.

Howard's Paternal Great Grandparents:
George Washington and Martha Ann Randall Henderson

George (1833-1927) born in Illinois, died in Bradgate-Martha (1840-1937) born in Mason City, died in Bradgate

Married in 1856–George came to Mason City as a pioneer in 1855 where he engaged in milling & lumber operations–Served more than 3 years in Union Army

One son and three daughters—Frank, Kate, Jem & Gail

One adopted son, a nephew of George Henderson, originally named Augustus Walters, was adopted in infancy following the death of his mother

The adopted son was renamed John Henderson—John Henderson was Howard's grandfather

George & Martha moved their family to Sac County, Iowa in 1875–In 1882 they homesteaded in Pocahontas County and established Highland Farm between Bradgate and Rolfe where they lived until death

George was a successful farmer and also served two years as State Senator of Iowa-Buried in Rolfe, Iowa

Howard's Paternal Grandparents:
John and Mattie Edna King Henderson

John (1876-1950) born in Kentucky, died in Bradgate-Mattie (1875-1959) born in Bradgate, died in Bradgate—Both buried in Union Cemetery, Humboldt, IA
Married April 13, 1898 at Rolfe, IA-John & Mattie farmed three years near Humboldt and thereafter lived their entire married life at Bradgate, spending 23 years on the same farm one mile north of Bradgate where one son and three daughters were all born and raised
Floyd was Howard's father

HOWARD HENDERSON'S FATHER'S MATERNAL ANCESTRY—THE KINGS

Howard's Paternal Great-Great-Great-Great Grandparents:
James and Deliverance Harriman King

James was born in England in 1728—He was forced into the English Navy as a young man by a "press gang" at the time of the French and Indian War
James and a shipmate deserted when sent on a quest for food when their ship was at Portsmouth, New Hampshire
They were befriended at Haverhill, Mass. after tunneling by night—He married a Haverhill girl named Deliverance Harriman in 1750
Two children, George and Jesse, were born at Hamstead, New Hampshire

Howard's Paternal Great-Great-Great Grandparents:
George and Mehitable Noyes King

About 1798 they moved to Orange, Vermont as early settlers where their eight children were born–One son, John Noyes King, was born in 1817–He was their youngest
George King died in 1835 at the age of 63—His widow then married his brother Jesse King

Howard's Paternal Great-Great Grandparents:
John Noyes and Martha Sweet King

John (1817-1881) and Martha (1822-1845)–Both born in Vermont–They had 3 children–Mary Jane, John Wesley & Edward R.
John Wesley King, Howard's great grandfather, was born in Belvidere, IL, November 1, 1841

Howard's Paternal Great Grandparents:
John Wesley and Ann Eliza Averill King

John (1841-1908) born in Illinois, died in Bradgate and Ann (1844-1931) born in Clockville, NY, died in Bradgate, both are buried in Union Cemetery, Humboldt, IA
Married on October 17, 1869 in Springvale (now Humboldt)
They had one son and five daughters—Frederick, Clara, Mattie, Bertha, Bessie, Maud
Mattie Edna King was born at Bradgate, August 25, 1875 and died at Bradgate, March 1, 1959—Buried in Union Cemetery at Humboldt
Mattie was Howard's grandmother—Howard's father's mother

HOWARD HENDERSON'S MOTHER'S PATERNAL ANCESTRY—THE HEMERSONS

Howard's Maternal Great Grandparents:
Nelson and Gunvor Felland Hemerson

Nelson (1824-1905) born in Bergen, Norway, died in Bradgate-Gunvor (1823-1916) born in Norway, died in Bradgate
Nelson came to Madison, Wisconsin in 1845, Gunvor in 1843–Gunvor married Ole Sanden in 1845–They had two children–Ole died in 1850

Nelson and Gunvor married in 1852 in Sun Prairie, Wisconsin–Four sons and four daughters were born–Gunder (Dave), Herman, Albert, Trena, Emma, Lettie, Julie, Rasmus

The first six were born in Sun Prairie, the other two at the Hemerson homestead in Humboldt County southeast of Bradgate, IA

The family moved to Humboldt County in 1869 where Nelson had homestead farmland at $3.25 per acre

Albert Hemerson was Howard's grandfather

Howard's Maternal Grandparents:
Albert and Eva Louisa Bell Howell Hemerson

Albert (1864-1956) born in Sun Prairie, died in Bradgate-Eva (1879-1967) born in Centerville, IA, died in Sheldon, IA

Married September 20, 1900 in Humboldt—they homesteaded farmland one mile east of Bradgate where all seven sons and two daughters were born

Albert and Eva Louisa were buried in Union Cemetery, Humboldt, IA

Alice was Howard's mother.

HOWARD HENDERSON'S MOTHER'S MATERNAL ANCESTRY—THE HOWELLS

Howard's Maternal Great-Great Grandparents:
Isaac and Eliza James Howell

Isaac (1825-1862)–Eliza James (1826-1858) were French Canadian Indians-Isaac died at age 37 (accident building home)–Eliza died at age 32 of Tuberculosis

Two sons—Paul Francis and George who became orphans at ages 7 and 9 and were then raised by the Wilbur family

Paul later married the Wilbur's daughter Silvia—they were Howard's great grandparents

Josiah and Louisa Carr Wilbur

Josiah (1823-1911) born in Ohio (parents born in Scotland)–Louisa (1827-1914) born in Pennsylvania (parents born in Germany)
They had seven daughters and two sons.
Sylvia was Howard's great grandmother

Howard's Maternal Great Grandparents:
Paul Francis Howell and Sylvia Wilbur Howell

Paul Francis (1855-1922) born in Eddyville IA, died Humboldt IA-Sylvia (1856-1943) born in Sandyville IA, died in Bradgate IA
Married April 2, 1874 at Indianolo IA
Nine sons and four daughters—Fred, Archie, Isaac, Edward, Ned, William, Benjamin, John, Paul Dewey, Eva Louisa, Estelle May, W. Ellen (Plucar), Emma.
Eva Louisa was Howard's grandmother.

Memoirs of
Howard Dale Henderson

Written
April 8, 1999

Born March 26, 1923, on a farm 2 miles east of Bradgate, Iowa at the home of my mother's Aunt Ellen (Howell) Plucar. Mrs. Plucar was the midwife for my birth. Lived on a farm near Bradgate most of the time through age 5. At about age 3 or 4 we lived on my mother's uncle Ed Howell's farm near Austin, Minnesota where my dad was a hired hand.

Lived in Gilmore City, Iowa in 1928 where I started school in the first grade. Finished 1st grade in a one-room country school near Pioneer, Iowa where we lived on a farm. At the Pioneer school, one teacher taught grades 1 through 8. Pioneer is near and SE of Gilmore City. One girl and I comprised the entire 1st grade. My dad was a farm hand and also worked on a railroad section gang.

In the late spring of 1929, we moved to Waterloo, Iowa where my dad had secured much needed employment at the John Deere Tractor Works where he had uninterrupted employment until his retirement in 1965. We initially lived on Columbia Street (east side), but moved to 739 Dundee where I started 2nd grade at Edison in the fall of 1929. Due to not ever attending kindergarten and a somewhat skimpy 1st grade education, I was not ready for 2nd grade at Edison. I was demoted one year and took the second half of 1st grade again. At that time, each grade was divided in two (B and A), so I was demoted from 2B to 1A. I went to Edison through part of 5th grade.

My mother obtained full time employment in the bacon department of the Rath Packing Co in about 1932 where she worked until a heart condition forced retirement in about 1942. The heart problem was due to continuing to play basketball in high school when she had rheumatic fever. My mother loved her job at Rath's and helped form and was secretary of the first independent labor union there. I passed out Union literature handbills to Rath plant workers as they entered the plant.

From the time I completed my first year of school in Waterloo in 1930 until I completed 11th grade in 1940, I spent every summer vacation on the farm at Bradgate. My mother's youngest brothers, Donald and Gordon Hemerson, were just 3 and 5 years respectively older than I. My older brother Bob and I had many great times at Bradgate during the summer vacations. The combination of older uncles and life on the farm facilitated early orientation of the facts of life.

From age 7 in 1930 through age 13 in 1936, I spent summer vacations on Grandpa and Grandma Hemerson's farm one mile east of Bradgate. Grandma Hemerson was over-burdened taking care of sons Russell, Noble, Lester, Gordon and Donald plus Bob, Beverly, Junior and I. There was no electricity, running water or inside plumbing. The cook stove was fueled with corncobs and wood. We called Grandpa and Grandma Hemerson, Ma and Dad the same as her sons did.

The West Branch of the Des Moines River ran through the Hemerson farm, so we had many fun times fishing and swimming. When we really needed to take a bath, we went to the river with a bar of soap.

We trapped pocket gophers for which the county paid a 5-cent bounty. We were quite proficient with slingshots and a 22-caliber rifle, shooting rats around the corncribs and striped gophers in the pasture. With our slingshots, we got birds and glass insulators on the telephone lines that ran along the railroad track which passed through the farm. Un-be-knownst to Grandma Hemerson, we chased her chickens as they tried to roost in the trees and barn. We also caught sparrows in the evening as they roosted under the eaves and in the straw stacks. I also remember playing catch with rotten eggs until they broke.

Along with the fun times, you were put to work at an early age at such chores as feeding animals, milking cows, gathering eggs, cutting weeds, pulling morning glories in the corn and gathering wild grapes for Grandpa's wine. There was an apple orchard and Grandpa Hemerson had a cider press, so that was kind of fun.

While most of the summertime was spent on the Hemerson farm, occasionally we stayed at Grandpa and Grandma Henderson's farm one mile north of Bradgate. Bob and I had good times at nearby Aunt Edna's farm with our cousins Gene and Dean Madsen. Aunt Edna is my dad's sister and is still alive at age 95. She was in the same class as my mother in high school.

From age 14 in 1937 through age 17 in 1940, I spent summer vacations working on the farm for Aunt Lucille and Uncle Teddy Lee. Lucille was my mother's younger sister and was only 8 years older than I. I treasure the four summers I spent with Lucille and Teddy. They had no children. I did my share of hard work cultivating corn, shocking and threshing oats plus lots of daily chores. Great food was plentiful all the time, and particularly during several weeks of threshing oats on a community type operation with several neighbors.

Gene Madsen, Howard Henderson, Bob Henderson, & Dean Madsen

We went to town at Bradgate, Monday, Wednesday and Saturday nights. Monday night was free outdoor movies. Aunt Lucille kidded me that when the loud music signaled the end of the movie, the young lovers suddenly came racing back from their secret places. Wednesday and Saturday nights Donald, Gordon, Bob and I quite often went to the dance at Rolfe seven miles away. I drank beer at the dances at about age 14 or 15. The cows got milked early Saturday evenings and late Sunday morning.

I learned to drive with a Model "A" Ford in the oat fields at Lucille and Teddy's farm. I was able to practice driving country roads when Donald used Uncle Noble's 1935 Ford for dates. Donald sat in the back seat with Virginia while giving me driving instructions.

Learning to drive Lucille and Teddy's Model "A" Ford coupe recalls another incident at age 14. They were renting Great Uncle Erasmus Hemerson's farm just west of Grandpa and Grandma Hemerson's farm. There was a huge hill behind the house. One evening Aunt Lucille was driving the F12 Formal tractor from the field, Teddy was driving the Model "A" and I was riding the running board. As we started down the big hill, Teddy became alarmed Lucille might tip over the tractor. He jumped out of the moving car thinking I could take over. I jumped off the running board, and down the hill went the driverless car. My worst fear was the car would hit the stock watering tank I had just hand pumped full. Fortunately it missed the tank and ran up the tongue of a nearby cultivator, which then came to rest against a woven wire fence, doing very little damage to the car or anything else. I showed Kirk, Heidi and Jean the farm site and hill when we were at Bradgate this year. The house and farm buildings are no longer there.

On that same farm the same year I acquired the scar behind my right hand thumb. I was in the field cultivating corn with a single row cultivator and a team of horses. The wooden peg holding one of the shovels broke when it struck a rock as it is supposed to. When I was pulling the shovel back in place to replace the wooden peg, my hand slipped and the sharp edge of the shovel put a big gash in my hand. I immediately headed for the house, and got the rest of the day off.

While working for Teddy and Lucille where Teddy now lives, I recall a humorous incident. I was told to bring the cows up from a pasture a half-mile from the farmhouse, but I was to leave the bull in the pasture. I got the cows out and left the bull okay, but as I was driving the cows up the lane, the bull crashed through the fence and came running. I thought he was after me so I ran. The bull went right by me to join the cows. No harm done. Kirk, Heidi and Jean were at this farm in 1998 also.

I could go on and on recalling great memories of summers on the farms at Bradgate. My mom and dad both worked full time and I rarely saw them during the 3-month summer vacations. Aunt Lucille died of ovarian cancer in 1959 at the age of 45. Uncle Teddy is still alive on this farm.

In 1933 we moved from the 739 Dundee Edison School district. I was part way through 5th grade. I guess my claim to fame at Edison was winning the marble tournament. Also, I fell in love with Betty Pickleman. We moved from 739 Dundee to 522 W9th where we were in the Lowell School district. Actually we made a move to the Emerson School district from 739 Dundee for one day. After we had moved into this large two-story apartment house, the landlord discovered the total number of kids, and we moved back to 739 Dundee the following day.

I finished 5th and 6th grade at Lowell. My main recollections at Lowell were being on the basketball team with a young lady coach named Miss Meyer who drove a Ford convertible, and my grade school sweetheart,

Mary Uban. I followed Mary around during recess tossing licorice cara-mels calling Fairy Wonders to her. I also remember my family teasing me when Mary Uban sent me a mushy valentine with a Chinese verse, which ended by saying *All a samie, I love you.* I kissed Mary Uban for the first time 50 years later at a class reunion.

In about 1935 we moved about one mile from 522 W 9th to 725 West 8th where we lived when I started 7th grade at Sloan Wallace Junior High. I was comfortable and got along quite well at Sloan Wallace where I partici-pated in basketball, football, softball and track.

In 1936 we moved less than a mile to 1102 Leavitt, and I continued school at Sloan Wallace, which was on Washington between W6th and W7th. My folks rented the house on Leavitt with an option to buy. They bought the 3 bedroom, 2-story house for $3,500—the first house they owned. My mother's brothers Lester, Gordon and Donald lived with us at different times at 1102 Leavitt. Lester worked at Deeres. Gordon and Donald attended Gates Business College. Gordon met his wife Beulah Sealock from Traer while living in Waterloo.

It was a disaster for me when in 1937 they changed the school bound-aries and I was forced to transfer from Sloan Wallace to West Junior High while in the 8th grade. At the time junior high was 7th, 8th and 9th grades. West Junior and West High shared the same building.

In 1937, at age 14, I narrowly escaped death following surgery for a very severely infected and rotted mastoid bone behind my right ear. The infection followed a bout with scarlet fever. This problem occurred shortly after my transfer to West Junior High, and didn't make the transition eas-ier.

I felt like a rebel from the time I transferred to West Junior High in 8th grade. This continued to varying degrees in high school grades 10 through 12 which was at the same location as West Junior High. It was not all bad, and I graduated from Waterloo West High School in January 1941 with a fairly decent scholastic record. Other than my love life and a few close friends, I don't have too many happy memories of high school.

I had a Des Moines Register route during the school year in 1935 and 1936, and was able to buy myself a very nice bicycle. It was colored orange and green, the colors of the Thunderbolt Club, an athletic club Bob and I were in.

Immediately following graduation from high school, I went to work as an optician lens grinder at $.30 per hour. As I lived at home on Leavitt with free room and board, I was able to buy a beautiful maroon 1939 Chevrolet for $500. I continued work as an optician lens grinder for just over two years at which time I volunteered for military service. I transferred to Oklahoma City for a few weeks with this same optical company. I did not take my 1939 Chevy, as it needed new tires, which were unavailable due to World War II rationing. I did not last long in Oklahoma City due to missing my girl friend, my family and my car. I had my mom sell my 1939 Chevy, and I bought a 1940 to drive home from Oklahoma City. Uncle Donald had just completed officer's training at Fort Sill, Oklahoma so I was able to give him a ride home.

Since my fellow workers, including my boss, all went to the military; I became the supervisor of the lens-grinding department at $.50 per hour. As such, I was given a few months deferment from military service.

I had a strong desire to become a fighter pilot, and made several attempts to enlist for training as such in both the Army and Navy air forces. They had a strong preference for people with college training. Finally in March of 1943, I made one final effort by volunteering for the Army, which at that time was the only way to get in the air force. I had to beg to be accepted in the Army because of flat feet. Ironically, I was unable to transfer to the air force due to being color blind, and to my horror, they put me in the Army infantry, flat feet and all. I was sent to Ft. Jackson near Columbia, South Carolina for basic training with the newly activated 106th Infantry Division. I was very fortunate to be assigned to the communications platoon of the battalion headquarters company. I became a member of the telephone wire squad. Our responsibility was to follow the battalion commander laying telephone wire so that whenever he chose we were to hand him a telephone to communicate with his rifle company commanders. When the battalion stopped to set up camp, we set up a switchboard and ran telephone service from battalion headquarters to the three rifle companies and the heavy weapons company. An infantry battalion consisted of about 900 people making up five companies. Three rifle companies, one heavy weapons company (machine guns) and battalion Headquarters Company.

Our one year of basic training included learning to climb telephone poles with spikes, firing the M-1 rifle, bayonet training, hand to hand combat and many 25 mile hikes with full field pack enduring the heat of South Carolina. It was work, but we had a lot of fun along the way. I was associated with many young men from the east and the south. I first heard of pizza from the easterners. They called it tomato pie. They were not impressed with the pizza we found in Columbia, South Carolina. The easterners also informed me of the existence of gay men, but they were known as queers in 1943. On one occasion, I was shocked when we roamed downtown Columbia in search of a "queer" to roll for money or jewelry. Fortunately we were unsuccessful.

During the first 6 weeks of basic training, I assumed greater responsibility when I became a corporal and was 2nd in command of the 10-man battalion telephone wire squad. I rather enjoyed giving the commands of close order drill. I recall a time of humor when one guy in our platoon was promoted to private 1st class and was told to give close order drill to a squad of men. As usual it was a very warm day so the newly promoted PFC marked time under a small shade tree while giving commands to the squad marching in the hot sun. He was immediately reduced back to the rank of buck private. On a few occasions, we had a full-blown dress parade whereby the entire infantry division of 3,000 men marched to music from loud speakers. This was impressive but hot in full dress carrying M1 rifles in the Carolina sun.

After a year of basic training, we departed Ft. Jackson for full field maneuvers in Tennessee. Maneuvers are field exercises of simulated actual combat conditions. Our 106th division fought a make believe war against another infantry division. One side wore red ribbons, the other side blue. By this time, I was a sergeant and was the battalion telephone wire squad leader with two jeeps at my disposal. We set up a switchboard at battalion headquarters and laid telephone lines to the headquarters of the three rifle companies and the heavy weapons company. We then had to maintain the telephone wires, which were laid on the ground off large spools mounted on the back of the jeeps. The wires quite often were damaged and we had to trace them down for repair. On occasion, we would have the switchboard operator yell out that a line was out when it wasn't. We would then take off in a jeep for a lark. One time we got lost behind "enemy" lines and ran short of gas. We stole a can of gas from the "enemy" in downtown Murfreesboro, Tennessee. After laying telephone wire for any training exercise, we had to rewind the wire onto the spools by hand.

It was winter in Tennessee, and the weather became miserable living in two-man pup tents. We had snow and rain. There were occasions that we hoped to get sick so we could go to the field hospital, but to no avail. One night my pup tent partner and I did not properly dig a trench around our tent and a heavy rain made a river through our tent. We spent the rest of the night in the company kitchen pyramidal tent. This reminds me that on maneuvers our headquarters company had its own kitchen. While in Ft. Jackson, we had to share a rifle company kitchen, and on several occasions we were shorted if something ran out-particularly dessert.

After weeks of Tennessee maneuvers, we were trucked to Camp Atterbury, Indiana near Indianapolis. I was very excited because now I was close enough to home in Waterloo to make it on a 3-day pass. It never happened, as all of a sudden I was on my way overseas to England.

The only time I got leave to go home was from Ft. Jackson, S.C. in September 1943. I traveled all night by bus, then hitchhiked to Cincinnati, flew from there to Chicago and then to Waterloo by train. By coincidence, Uncle Donald was also home on leave. I went to Ft. Dodge to help Donald bring Virginia and their first daughter Judy home to Bradgate.

At Camp Atterbury our 106th Division was almost completely decimated. Most of us were split away from those we had trained with for 14 months, and were shipped overseas as replacements in May 1944. I felt like an orphan for most of the next year. This may have been a real stroke of luck as the revised 106th Infantry Division left the states many months later and was wiped out at the "Battle of the Bulge" in December 1944.

That reminds me while with the 106th Division training in the field we lived on bag lunches. We referred to ourselves as the "hungry and sick bag lunch division". *(Compiler's note: It was many times through before noticing how '106th' sounds so much like 'hungry and sick.')*

I traveled out of Boston Harbor by liberty ship and arrived in England May 12, 1944, 25 days prior to D-Day. Again luck was with me, as I did not participate in D-Day. There were many fellow replacement soldiers picked at random to be dropped by gliders into Normandy, and most were wiped out or captured. It didn't make any difference what you had been trained for; they just needed bodies—anyone who could fire an M1 or a carbine.

I was in England living in a pyramidal tent taking light training for a few weeks. I did get to London. Black and white American soldiers were not allowed in town the same night. The English girls had no preference, and this caused problems. The U.S. was not integrated at that time.

One night late in June I was herded aboard ship with other replace-ments to sail across the English Channel. We sailed out of Portsmouth, England heading straight about 100 miles to Normandy, certainly not the shortest route. I remember playing poker on the way. We waded ashore from landing craft on the beaches of Normandy. My luck held again—nobody was shooting at us.

We marched several miles inland and set up camp a few miles from St. Lo where the Germans were heavily entrenched and fortified. I lived alone there in a covered foxhole for many days. We were in a replacement camp behind the front lines. The Allies were waiting for a clear day for the air force to blast the Germans out of their St. Lo fortress. We just killed time and played softball in the small fields between the hedgerows. One night there was a false alarm gas attack. Many soldiers had discarded their gas masks, and you can imagine the crying. One night I went to retire in my foxhole and discovered I had company—a cat. Finally an allied air armada of 3,000 planes flew over us for what seemed like hours and leveled the town of St. Lo. Even so, some of the Germans survived.

We then moved out and embarked for Paris about 180 miles away. I have no recollection of how long it took to reach Paris. I do remember dead German soldiers and animals rotting along the roadsides.

At some point on the way to Paris I met a fellow Iowa farmer from Dayton named Floyd Magnuson. Floyd and I became 2 man pup tent buddies as we traveled by convoy on through Paris and towards Belgium. After setting up camp north of Paris, Floyd and I decided we wanted to see more of Paris. We went AWOL and hitchhiked to Paris for a short stay. Cigarettes and C rations would buy anything.

Our replacement outfit had moved on before we returned, but we found them and nobody knew we had been gone. Floyd and I played a lot of gin rummy in our dug in two-man pup tent to pass the time. I don't remember whether we were together weeks or months or what time of year we parted. I know I left St. Lo in July and was in Heerlen, Holland some 400 miles away by December 1944. I lost track of time in between.

At some point between Paris and Liege, Belgium, Floyd and I parted company from the replacement outfit as I was transferred to the 29th Infantry Division. However, instead of being assigned to a battalion head-quarters company telephone wire squad, I went to the 116th Regiment rehabilitation and replacement training center. This operation had been established to rehabilitate soldiers suffering minor wounds or mental problems from combat exhaustion. There was a psychiatric as well as medical staff. After it had been set up as a rehab center, it also became a center to receive incoming replacements some of which were retrained for front line assignments other than their previous training.

I was informed I was to be retrained as a rifle squad leader, which were in great demand for obvious reasons. This did not appeal to me, so I went to visit the commanding officer. He agreed there should be a need for my specialty so I escaped the rifle squad leader nightmare.

I stayed on for a considerable time at the combat exhaustion rehab and replacement training center to the point of becoming very bored. I went to the center's headquarters seeking things to do. I had some bookkeeping and typing experience from high school, so a Lt. Fitzgerald latched on to me for much needed clerical help. Lt. Fitzgerald was the 2nd in command, adjutant of the entire center. We got along well and he eventually made me the acting 1st sergeant of the whole operation. He said there was a move underway authorizing a permanent 1st sergeant position, which would give me a 3-step promotion. Unfortunately that never transpired, but that was of small consequence since I had a nice soft job for a while.

From Liege, Belgium, we went to Maastricht and Heerlen in Holland. In Heerlen we moved into a bombed out hotel with no water or electricity. We were there for weeks, and I became acquainted with some Dutch girls. I have some pictures, and remember Rosa whose father owned a shoe factory.

While in Heerlen in December 1944, we were trucked to a mine for showers. While dressing, I spotted soldiers wearing 7th Armored Division patches. I inquired as to whether they knew Lt. Hemerson. Since the 7th Armored included some 3,000 men, it was a miracle these men were from Uncle Donald's company of 200. I boarded the truck with them and went to spend the evening with Donald. Unfortunately, Donald's outfit received emergency orders the next day to depart for duty in the "Battle of the Bulge" some 30 or 40 miles south.

Having reached the age of 21 in 1944, while at Heerlen, I voted for Franklin Delano Roosevelt for president in the November elections.

Shortly after seeing Uncle Donald, we moved on some 25 miles to Aachen, Germany. We occupied houses in this small village for at least a month while the Battle of the Bulge lasted from December 16, 1944 to January 16, 1945. At Aachen the allies spent part of the winter camped on one side of the Roer River while the Germans were on the other side.

We moved from Aachen about 40 miles to Munchen-Gladback, from there 20 miles to Düsseldorf, and then about 25 miles to an area north of Duisburg, Germany. While in Munchen-Gladback, a German woman reported an American soldier had raped her. I had to line up our entire outfit to see if she could identify the guilty party. Fortunately she was unable to identify him because in wartime rape was a death penalty offense.

About the time we were just north of Duisburg, I was finally transferred from the 29th Division rehabilitation and replacement training center to a permanent assignment in a battalion headquarters company telephone wire squad. We moved some 240 miles from north of Duisburg to Magdeburg on the Elbe River. This move was quite rapid as the Germans were on the run. We captured many young kids as well as old men. We met up with our Russian allies at the Elbe River as the war in Europe ended May 8, 1945. We were 70 miles from Berlin. As we moved through Germany, we quite often occupied houses in the German towns. We usually picked out the nicer homes. Many of the homes had wine cellars, so this was one of the perks of war. When we entered Germany, our commanding general supposedly said anything we saw and wanted was ours. I guess each of us had his own interpretation of limitations.

I have highlighted my travels from Portsmouth, England to Duisburg, Germany on page 108 of our Great World Atlas. Duisburg to Magdeburg is shown on page 104.

From Magdeburg, I traveled more than 400 miles to Fontainebleau, France, 35 miles south of Paris, to attend an 8-week officer's training school. The school was established to replace rifle platoon leaders who were quite expendable in the European theater of operations. Even though the war had ended, we had already been designated for the school. We were the last class. While at Fontainebleau, we were allowed to spend a few weekends in Paris.

We were commissioned 2nd lieutenants in July 1945, and were then slated to be sent to battle the Japanese in the Pacific theater of operations. I was lucky to have earned enough points in the European war to get to visit home before going on to the Pacific. Some of my fellow officers were to go directly.

While awaiting the ship to travel from Le Havre, France to the U.S., the Japanese surrendered. I arrived in New York Harbor greatly exhilarated to see the Statue of Liberty in August 1945. I not only escaped the Pacific war, I got home earlier than I otherwise would have due to accepting the commission as 2nd Lt. My good fortune continued.

Following my discharge from the army, I enrolled for the fall quarter of UNI in November 1945. I arranged morning classes so I was done with studies early afternoon. A group of us, including Bob Schreiner, Bill Gardner, Al Welbes and Mike Murphy, met regularly afternoons at the "office" (Hi Ho Lounge).

Jean and I had our first date on her 19th birthday, December 5, 1945. We met in English class at UNI, and it was love at first sight. We lived only 3 blocks apart in Waterloo at 914 Grant and 1102 Leavitt. I ran a daily taxi service to UNI including Jean, Bob Schreiner, Al Welbes and Al's brother-in-law, Joe Doyle.

It was fun times during my 2 quarters at UNI. UNI was on the quarter system at that time, and offered very limited accounting courses.

I enrolled at the University of Iowa the fall semester of 1946 where I majored in accounting. I worked on the assembly line at Deere's in the summer of 1946. At the U of I, I lived in the Hillcrest Dormitory. My roommate was Mike Murphy, and Bob Schreiner and Al Welbes also roomed together there. We played penny-ante poker nearly every evening, and seldom left the dormitory at night. None of us had a car, but we managed to hitch a ride to Waterloo most weekends.

I gave Jean a fur-trimmed coat for Christmas in 1946, and my friends concocted a story that I bought her a fur coat with my poker winnings.

Jean and I were married April 3, 1947 during spring break. Bob Schreiner was my best man and Bill Gardner and Al Welbes were ushers. Mike Murphy was unable to participate due to nose surgery. For a wedding present, Mike, Al and Bob gave us a set of stainless steel silverware collected from the Hillcrest Dormitory cafeteria. We honeymooned in St. Louis using my folks new 1947 Chevy. Cars were still rationed so I used my veteran's priority to get the car. I sold my folks' 1940 Oldsmobile to a newly graduated doctor for $1,025, which was more than it cost new. That car would cost more than $20,000 in 1998.

Jean and I initially lived in a very small two room apartment on the 2nd floor of an old house at 416 S. Clinton in Iowa City. The converted closet kitchen was so small you stood outside of it in our living room rather than in it. The bed touched three walls in the bedroom. We shared a refrigerator and bathroom in the hallway. There were also students in the basement and attic. By coincidence, Bob and Joan Schreiner later lived in the attic apartment.

We had no car, so Jean and I hitchhiked to Waterloo a couple times while she was pregnant with Julie. I went to summer school in 1947, and in the early fall we moved into a new 2 bedroom barracks near the U of I hospital. The barracks were built to house married veterans, and to us at that time were luxurious. I used my flat feet as priority to get one of the few with wooden floors. We had an icebox so I drilled a hole in the floor for a funnel to drain the water. Later we got a used refrigerator. Our rent was $30 per month including heat and electricity.

Later in 1947 we bought a 1930 Model "A" Ford for $125. It was in excellent condition with low mileage, so we drove it from Iowa City to Waterloo. As a veteran on the GI Bill, I received my tuition, books and fees plus $110 per month, the equivalent of ten times that much now. We got by quite nicely.

Julie was born October 8, 1947. As a low-income veteran, we qualified for state assistance. As a student wife, Jean had prenatal doctor care at the U of I hospital at no cost. The labor pains came in the middle of the night and we walked from our barracks to the hospital. Julie was born the next morning. Jean had to share a ward with other state patients, but it was entirely at no cost to us. Both grandmothers spent time with us to help Jean with Julie.

Julie developed a low hemoglobin blood condition and also had to wear a cast temporarily to correct one foot, which was slightly turned at the ankle. These two conditions required several visits at the U of I children's hospital, which was only about a block from our barracks. They were able to completely rectify both problems.

I received my BS degree in accounting in August 1948 after attending summer school. With the combination of some credits for World War II service and 2 summer sessions, I earned my degree in less than 3 years. I received a letter of commendation from U of I President Virgil Hancher stating I graduated with high distinction for having a superior scholastic record, and I was elected to Beta Gamma Sigma national honorary society.

I had job offers from Shaeffer Penn in Ft. Madison and Burroughs and Cherry Burrel in Cedar Rapids, but we decided we wanted to return to Waterloo. After taking every accounting course offered at U of I except those specifically for public accounting, I accepted a job with a CPA named Charlie Hostetler. Since two years public accounting was required to take the CPA test, the pay was terrible. So, after graduating with honors, I went to work for $225 a month—that's $2,700 per year. However, the plus side was that Charlie Hostetler was a lone practitioner, so I learned every aspect of public accounting in the 27 months at that job. I passed my CPA exam in November 1950.

Our first home in Waterloo was a fairly decent first floor apartment in a house at 2149 Lafayette, but we had to share a bath with another couple.

While living on Lafayette, Suzanne Claire was born December 16, 1948. We stayed with Jean's folks at 914 Grant for a few days when Jean and Sue were discharged from Allen Hospital. That is when tragedy struck. Julie Ann was 14 months old and walking quite efficiently. She suddenly grabbed a pickle dish off the dinner table and fell on it, piercing her eyeball. I rushed her to the Presbyterian Hospital 3 blocks away, but she did not survive the anesthesia. They termed it an anesthetic death, but we were never convinced there was not carelessness involved. We were devastated and bitter. I remember evenings crying as we took walks from our Lafayette apartment. Having Sue to care for was our only salvation. Julie's death was the only time I can remember seeing my dad cry.

We moved to a fairly nice upstairs 2-bedroom apartment at 411½ Denver in 1950. We had the entire upstairs of a two-story house with our own private entrance and bath for $45 per month including heat. We sold our 1930 Model "A" Ford for $125, the same as we paid in 1947 and bought a new 1950 Chevrolet. We lived at 411½ Denver until 1953. While living on Denver, a neighbor volunteered an old set of clubs, and I took up the game of golf. For a number of years, I enjoyed twice week golf with a foursome including Frank Olson, Chuck Smith and Wayne Gaddis. We played at Byrnes and Gates. I wish the same foursome were still playing together now. After Wayne Gaddis died in about the mid 1960's, Don McLaughlin and Verne Nilsson played with us.

I decided public accounting was not for me and quit in October 1950. I then had no income to support Jean, Sue and myself. My philosophy was I needed to find new, full time work. I thought I was an income tax expert and could find temporary work at Carney, Alexander and Lynch CPA firm during the tax season. I was shocked and declined when they offered $1.00 per hour. In desperation, I took a job in the plant of Titus Mfg., but was there less than a week when I started at Chamberlain, November 16, 1950.

Chamberlain advertised for an experienced standard cost accountant to start up a standard cost accounting system which had been designed by an expert from their public accounting firm Bigelow, Kent and Willard. Chamberlain was not successful in finding the person they were looking for, so they hired me. I took the position not knowing the salary, and was pleased to find the pay was $325 per month compared to the $235 I was making after over 2 years in public accounting. I liked the new job and had no problem grasping the standard cost accounting system we installed to track costs in the washing machine wringer and aluminum refrigerator shelf products manufactured at Chamberlain.

Chamberlain had been in the defense contract business in both World Wars II, and I and had defense research and development contracts when I started work there. Early on, I took over the R&D defense contract accounting in addition to the standard cost system of wringers and shelves. Alas, I finally found my niche!! I assumed the responsibility of maximizing the share of overhead costs recovered on the R&D defense contracts. This involved dealing with and negotiating costs with government auditors. From the R&D contracts, I eventually branched out to the defense production contracts. That proved to be the making of a major portion of my 39+ year career at Chamberlain. War provided my college education and my career.

We were thrilled when Kirk Richard was born at Allen Hospital August 20, 1952. Dr. Siebert said, "You have a beautiful 8 lb. redheaded boy." Prior to that time, my mother had been having serious mental problems and was at the mental health center at Independence when Kirk was born. From there I took her by ambulance to a private mental health clinic in Des Moines where she died October 8, 1952. She never got to see Kirk.

My mother's mental health situation was due to the lack of oxygen reaching her brain, which resulted from a major heart condition. The heart problem was discovered while she worked at Rath's. It was caused by rheumatic fever when she was in high school. The seriousness of it was not diagnosed and she was back in school playing basketball before adequately recovering. She resented having to limit her activities for 10 years prior to the mental problems. She was at Allen Hospital for a rest at the time Julie died. I think the shock had a major impact on her mental health. My dad was unable to cope with her prolonged mental illness, and was the one who had her committed to Independence. To avoid having the sheriff forcefully transport her, my sister Beverly and I somewhat deceptively took her to Independence and left her. I have ever since regretted doing so. Her condition deteriorated immediately. They were unable to treat her mental problem due to the heart condition.

We bought our first house at 1453 Bertch in 1953 for $14,500, and it served us well until 1960 when we moved to 234 Ivanhoe Rd. We sold the house on Bertch ourselves for $14,500 the same as we paid. One reason we moved was at that time it was planned W11th Street right next to us was to become an expressway and Bertch would become a major one-way access street. That plan was altered as Highway 21 was constructed but it did not come through to W11th.

While living on Bertch, we purchased a lot in the 200 block of Byron to build a house. We sold the lot when plans for a shopping center across the street were announced.

Good fortune came our way when Jane Elizabeth was born September 1, 1956. All three of our children were born in an election year at Allen Hospital, and were delivered by Dr. Cecil Seibert.

Sue and Kirk started kindergarten at Lowell in 1954 and 1957 respectively while we lived at 1453 Bertch. Jane started kindergarten at Kingsley in 1961 when we lived at 234 Ivanhoe Rd. Sue and Kirk also went to Kingsley through 6th grade.

My mother's brother Russell Hemerson died tragically from suicide in 1959 at the age of 54. Her only sister Lucille Lee died of cancer the same year at age 45. Having lived with and worked for Lucille and Teddy Lee for 4 years during summer vacations, Lucille was combination 2nd mother and sister to me. As Jean, Sue, Kirk and Jane are well aware, Bradgate was a very significant part of my life.

I spent a great amount of time at Chamberlain in Waterloo from 1950 to 1973 at which time Jean, Jane and I moved to Glen Ellyn, Illinois when I transferred to Chamberlain's corporate headquarters. For many years in Waterloo, I took on a 2nd job keeping the Chamberlain cafeteria books. This provided added income. Sue helped with the cafeteria books and payroll. I did bookkeeping for Pearson's Black Hawk Seed Farms in LaPorte City and Johnson's Hatchery on University Ave. I also did tax work, and Jean and I did a Sunday country paper route for $7 a week including gas. Jean's father Cliff Dryden died in May 1960 from heart disease at age 75.

In 1962 semi-pro hockey came to Waterloo with Oakey Brum, Emery Ruelle, Bernie Nielson, Butch Leskin, Bud McRae, Bill Dobbyn, Chris Batley, Dave Swick, Jimmy Coyle, Gordie Yewman, Jimmy Smith, Elof Seger, Mike White, etc. Our entire family was quite involved in the hockey operation for nearly 10 years. Sue became a cheerleader and assisted me with the payroll and bookkeeping while I was the treasurer. The Gay Blade room is a pleasant memory.

We moved to 3441 Rosehill Terrace in 1971. Sue married Tom Brand that year, and moved to Huntsville, Alabama where Tom trained with the Green Berets.

While living on Rosehill Terrace, Jane became the proud owner of an Arabian horse named Lady. Much to everyone's surprise, Lady foaled a colt named Hotshot. No one knew about it until it happened.

Sue graduated from Waterloo West High School in 1967, and enrolled at UNI. Kirk finished at West High in 1970, and attended UNI. In 1972, Kirk bought a new Ford Econoline van and moved to North Carolina to establish residence before enrolling at the University of North Carolina in Chapel Hill. He worked at construction there for a year before enrolling at UNC.

After 23 years at Chamberlain in Waterloo where I was division controller, I transferred to Chamberlain Corporate Headquarters in Elmhurst, Illinois in 1973. We moved from 3441 Rosehill Terrace to 23W285 Westchester Court in Glen Ellyn, Illinois in June of 1973. Leaving Waterloo to begin a new life was very traumatic. Jane had one year of high school left which she completed at Glenbard South in 1974. She then enrolled at UNI and moved back to Waterloo. She never moved back home, and was married to Stan Allen in 1976 in Waterloo. They met at UNI.

To gain familiarity with Chamberlain's 12 division operations in 7 different states, I reluctantly accepted the position of manager of internal audit. Fortunately, I reported to John Summers who let me very independently pick and choose my assignments. It was good experience with a fair amount of travel. I performed many special assignments.

After two years of internal audit, I became assistant corporate controller. Since I was then considered to be a company officer, I got my first company car.

Sue had too much time alone in Huntsville, so she returned to Waterloo in 1972 to continue at UNI. Tom was discharged from the service in 1973 and he then enrolled at UNI. We were extremely proud when Sue obtained her degree at UNI in 1973. Tom got his degree at UNI in 1975, and he and Sue moved to Downers Grove when Tom got a job in downtown Chicago with the Government as a Social Security Benefit Authorizer. Sue went to work for a small advertising firm in Chicago named Huwen and Davies in 1975, and is still there as part owner. Sue never took accounting courses in college, but she has worked in accounting almost entirely since, including time at KWWL television in Waterloo.

Kirk received a degree in English from UNC in 1975, and returned to Waterloo. He met Terri Roe at UNI in 1976, and they were married in LeMars on my birthday, March 26th, 1977. We got to use the Chamberlain company plane so Sue, Tom, Jean and I flew from Chicago to Waterloo where we picked up Jane and Stan, and then onto LeMars for the wedding. This was a treat for all of us. Kirk got a Chicago job with the government as Social Security Benefit Authorizer, and he, Terri and Heidi moved to Glen Ellyn shortly after Heidi was born August 30, 1977. They lived with us a few months before getting an apartment in Lisle.

Heidi Gene Henderson

In 1976, Chamberlain teamed with Mason Hanger Corp. of Lexington, Kentucky and was successful in winning a government contract to build a government-owned 155MM projectile plant at the NASA location near Bay St. Louis, Mississippi. The purpose of the new plant was to manufacture 155MM projectiles and grenades and to load, assemble and pack the finished item ready for combat. Previously Chamberlain manufactured only the projectile for shipment to a loading plant to be loaded, assembled and packed by other contractors. This was the 1st government venture to manufacture, load, assemble and pack at one location. Mason-Chamberlain was the name of the new corporation. They were to build a facility from scratch in a then Mississippi swamp, capable of producing 120,000 M483, 155MM projectiles and 10,560,000 grenades loaded, assembled and packed per month. The M483 projectile was a carrying round with 88 individual grenades in each projectile. Each grenade had a charge capable of destroying personnel as well as motor vehicles. The projectile had a range of up to 12 miles. After firing, while in flight, a time fuse would blow out the aluminum base plug of the projectile disbursing the 88 grenades. The grenades would float by individual tiny parachutes to the target exploding upon contact. A cut-a-way life-size sample of the grenade is on display in our basement. It took several years to build the plant, which was formally dedicated by ceremony in 1983. This entailed many challenges in the making, but was also very satisfying. Ironically, in the early 1990's, the government decided they no longer needed the M483 and shut the plant down. It is still maintained in idleness if and when it might be needed.

While at Chamberlain Corporate Headquarters, Jean and I participated in the weeklong annual management meetings from 1974 through 1980. These entailed winter trips to Jamaica, Florida, Nogales and San Marcus, Arizona and Houston, Texas. Our new owner discontinued the management meetings after 1980.

In 1979, Chamberlain was acquired by Dick Duchossois who had accumulated $100 million undivided profits in the 1970's by building railroad cars at Thrall Car in Chicago Heights, IL. Thrall Car was founded by Dick Duchossois's father-in-law named Thrall, but was merely a small railcar repair operation prior to Dick taking over after his World War II military service. Dick married Beverly Thrall who died of cancer about the time he acquired Chamberlain.

Owners of Chamberlain common stock were paid $30 per share for stock, which had cost us $.75, so the takeover was not all bad. There were changes made, but more good than bad. The corporate upstairs executive officers were luxuriously redecorated, and the one King Air 190 airplane was upgraded for a Citation II jet, plus a Gulfstream III jet and a helicopter were added.

Sometime after acquiring Chamberlain, Duchossois Industries Inc. was formed to include Chamberlain and Thrall Car. Duchossois Industries Inc. then moved from Chicago Heights to Chamberlain Headquarters in Elmhurst, IL.

Shortly thereafter, Chamberlain was split into two corporations. The 10 defense divisions became Chamberlain Mfg. Corp., and the 7 consumer divisions became Chamberlain Consumer Group Inc. This change brought about my happiest and most rewarding years of employment at Chamberlain. I became Vice President and Corporate Controller of Chamberlain Mfg. Corp. reporting to John Bergstrom who became President. Our corporate staff then consisted of John Bergstrom, Ed Smith, Frank Nipper and myself. Ed Smith was Vice President of all manufacturing operations, and Frank Nipper was VP of defense marketing operations. The four of us often traveled together to the 10 operating divisions, which included Mason Chamberlain Corp. in Mississippi. Many times we played gin rummy on the company plane enroute to and from.

I have said many times that I had the best job at Chamberlain the last 10 years prior to retirement December 31, 1989.

Jane and Stan moved to Worthington, MN in 1977 when Stan took a job at Hy-Vee Foods. Amy Sue was born in Worthington, April 16, 1978. The Allen's next moved to Faribault, MN where Stan managed the Hy-Vee deli. Brian Stanley was born in Faribault, April 30, 1980.

In 1982, the Allen's moved to Omaha, NE where Stan was HyVee deli manager. Kimberly Ann was born in Omaha December 26, 1982.

Amy, Brian, and Kimberly Allen

I retired from Chamberlain as of December 31, 1989. Craig Duchossois hosted a retirement party for me at the Meadow Club. Family attendees included Sue, Kirk, Jane and Stan. Tom Brand also attended. It was a most memorable occasion. A roving photographer took pictures all evening, and prepared an album for me.

During my first year of retirement, I worked for Chamberlain as a consultant. Most of the 36 days I worked were at the Mason Chamberlain plant in Mississippi, which I enjoyed.

We purchased the house at 618 Sheridan in Waterloo in July 1990, and moved from Glen Ellyn, IL October 2, 1990.

The family has had many fishing vacations in Canada and golf vacations in Hawaii. Jean and I have wintered in Inverness, FL every year starting in 1989 before I retired. Sue, Kirk, Terri, Jane, Stan, Heidi, Amy, Brian, Kim, Polly, Jim, Bob, B. Jo, Donald and Virginia have spent time with us there.

And you know the rest of the story.

978-0-595-37791-6
0-595-37791-2